Contents

Welcome to Rise and Shine Towers

1 🎧 0.04a **Listen and point.**

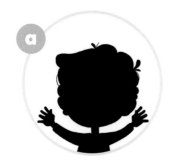
a

b

c

d

2 🎧 0.04b ✏️ **Listen and color. Then say.**

1   2   3   4   5

6   7   8

Tell me!

9   10

What's your favorite color? Tell a friend.

Extra time?

3   Find, circle, and color. Then say.

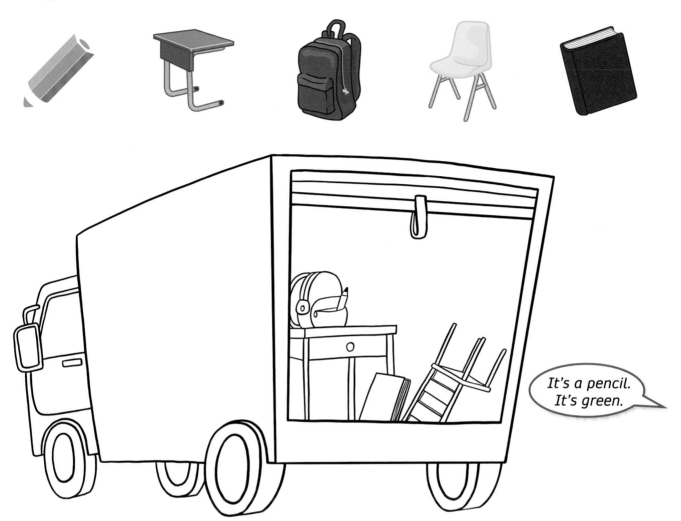

It's a pencil.
It's green.

 I can shine!

4   Draw for you.
Then say.

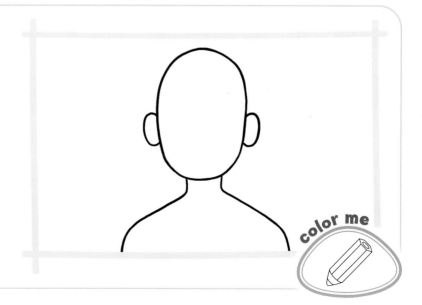

color me

Say the numbers 1–10.

Extra time?

Old toys, new toys

Lesson 1 ➡ Vocabulary

Let's review! | SB p6 ➡ **Find and color. Then say.**

1 Match and say.

Tell me!

Say the words in alphabetical order.

Extra time?

1 🎧 1.06 Listen and circle.

1 a b

2 a b

3 a b

4 a b

2 🎧 1.06a Listen and say *Yes* or *No*.

 I can shine!

3 ✏️ 💬 Color a toy in Activity 2.
Then tell a friend.

color me

1 `SB p12–13` ➡ **Which toy is new? Point and say *Yes* or *No*.**

2 ✏ **Find and color. Then say.**

Let's imagine! ✏

I can shine! ✳✳

3 ✏ **Draw. Then say.**

And you? What's your favorite toy at school?

color me

Rate the story and tell a friend. ☆☆☆   **Extra time?**

1 Which toy is big? Circle and say.

1

2

2 Follow, find, and say.

Let's build!

3 ✏ Complete, color, and say.

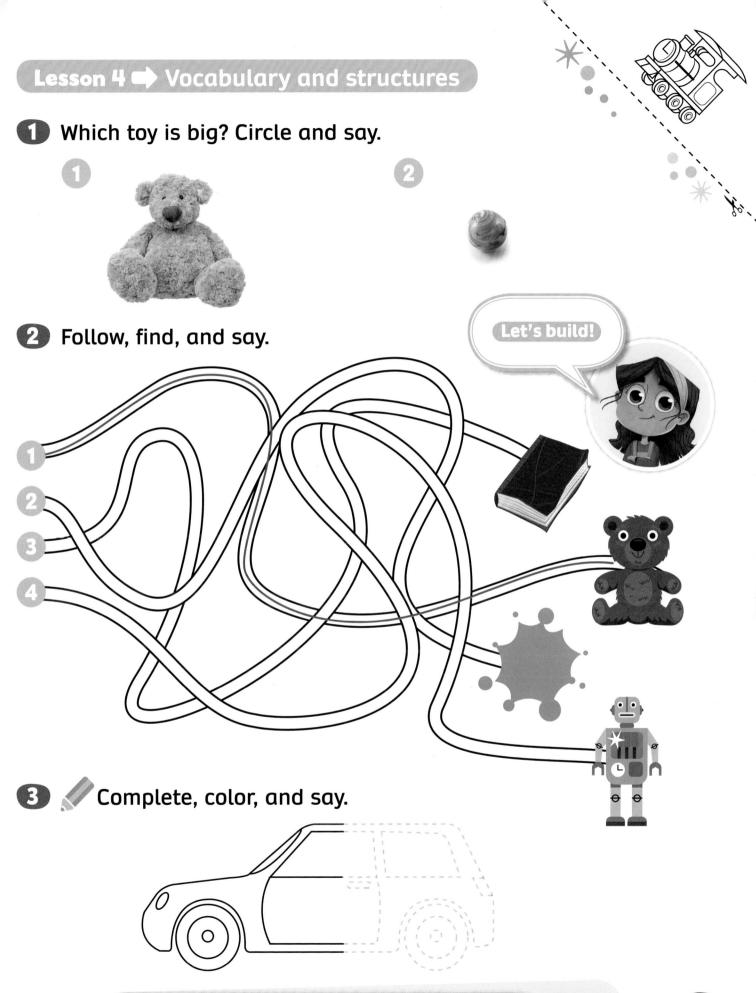

Think of an old toy you have. Draw and share with a friend.

1 🎧 1.13 ✏️ Listen and color.

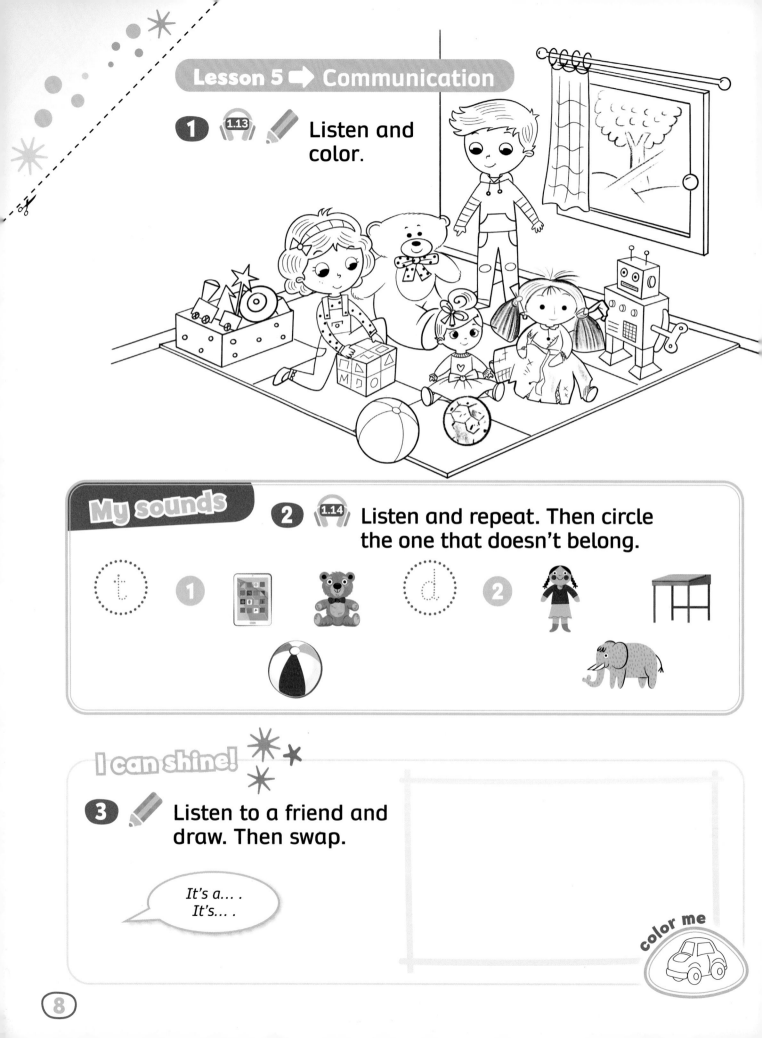

My sounds

2 🎧 1.14 Listen and repeat. Then circle the one that doesn't belong.

t   **1**

d   **2**

I can shine!

3 ✏️ Listen to a friend and draw. Then swap.

It's a... .
It's... .

color me

1 Find and circle the one that doesn't belong. Then say.

It's a new doll.

 **I can shine!**

Think and share

2 💬 Look, ask, and answer. Then role-play.

What's this?

It's a car.

color me

What toys do your friends share with you? Talk with a friend.

Extra time?

9

1 Look, match, and say.

1 2 3 4 5 6 7 8

a b c d e f g h

2 🖍 💬 Choose a toy. Is it new, old, big, or small?
Draw and color. Then tell a friend.

*It's a big car.
It's red.*

Do you put a teddy bear in a big box or a small box?

Extra time?

3 ✂️ ✏️ 💬 **Stick, draw, and color.**
Then play the game.

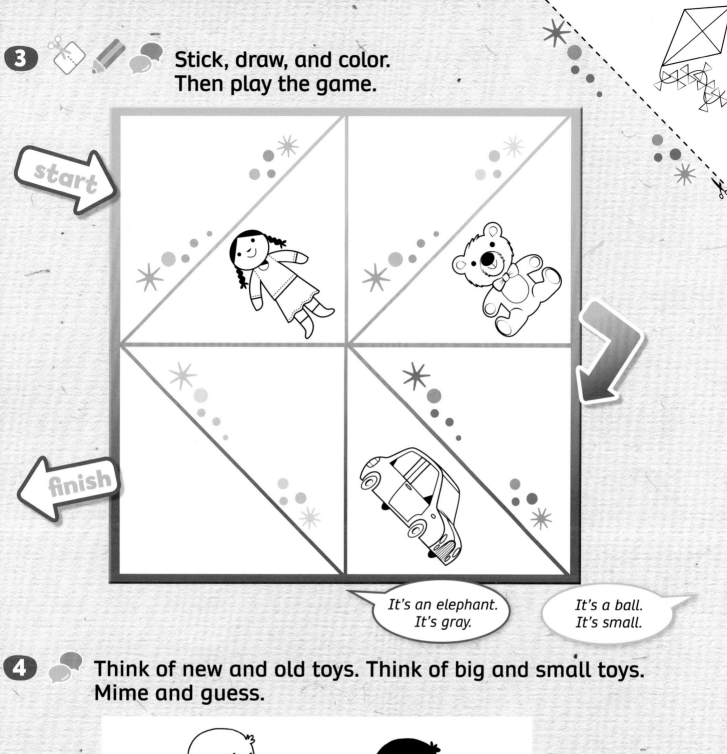

It's an elephant.
It's gray.

It's a ball.
It's small.

4 💬 **Think of new and old toys. Think of big and small toys.**
Mime and guess.

Make a toy box. Then show and tell your family.

⬇️ **Home-school link**

2 All kinds of families

Let's review!

SB p10–11 ➡ Find and color. Then say.

1 Match and say.

Tell me!

a

b

Say the words in alphabetical order.

Extra time?

1 🎧 2.06 **Listen and match.**

This is my family.

2 **Look at Activity 1. Describe and guess.**

I can shine!

3 ✏️ 💬 **Draw two people in your family. Then tell a friend.**

This is my grandma.

color me

Say your favorite family word.

Extra time?

1  **Who is in Bruno's family? Point and say *Yes* or *No*.**

2 **Follow. Then say.**

Let's imagine!

I can shine!

3 ✏️ **Draw. Then say.**

And you? Who's in your family?

color me

Rate the story and tell a friend. ☆☆☆

Extra time?

1 Listen and circle.

1

2

3

2 Match and say.

Let's build!

Think of a pet for you. Draw and share with a friend.

Extra time?

15

1 🎧 **2.13** Listen and point.

My sounds

2 🎧 **2.14** Listen and repeat. Then point and say.

I can shine!

3 💬 Circle for you. Then tell a friend.

I have a... . And you?

color me

1 Listen, point, and say.

This is for my cousin.

a

b

c

d

I can shine!

Think and share

2 Draw. Then tell a friend.

Who do you help in your family? Tell a friend.

Extra time?

17

1 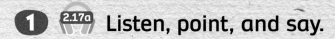 Listen, point, and say.

 a

 b

 c

 d

 e

 f

 g

 h

2   Listen and match. Then match for you. Tell a friend.

1

2

3

a

b

c

d

How many cousins do you have?

Extra time?

3 Stick, draw, and color. Then complete the family tree.

4 Think and draw for you. Then tell a friend.

Make a photo album page. Then show and tell your family.

Review 1 Important to me

1 🖍 Color and say.

It's a train.

2 🎧 2.19 💬 Listen and point. Then ask and answer.

a   b   c   d   e

Who's this?   This is my... .   What's this?   It's a... .

3 🖍 Color, point, and say.

1   2

4 **What do you have? Listen, circle, and say.**

5 🖊 **Think of a toy to play with. Draw and say.**

Let's play with the car!

Mini-project

6 🖊 **Think of a toy to give to your best friend. Draw and say.**

Time to shine!

7 🖊 **Look, think, and color.**

1

2

3

3 Amazing bodies

Lesson 1 ➡ Vocabulary

Let's review! | SB p20–21 ➡ | Find and color. Then say.

1 Match and say.

Tell me!

a

b

22

Say the words in alphabetical order.

Extra time?

1 3.06 🎧 **Listen and circle.**

1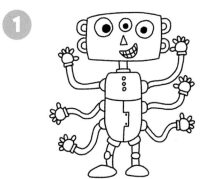

2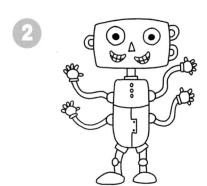

3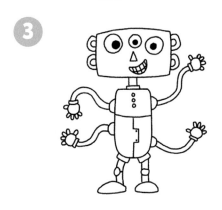

4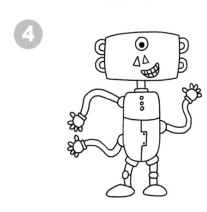

2 **Look at Activity 1. Describe and guess.**

I can shine!

3 🖊 💬 **Draw your robot. Then tell a friend.**

color me

1 SB p34–35 **Which is the one that doesn't belong?**
Point and say *Yes* **or** *No*.

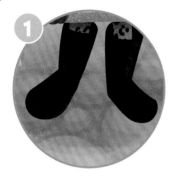 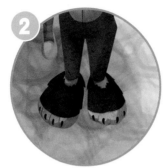  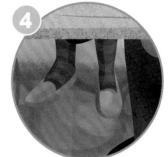

2 **Find and color. Then say.**

Let's imagine!

I can shine!

3 **Draw. Then say.**

And you?
Can you dance?

color me

Rate the story and tell a friend. ☆☆☆

Extra time?

1 🎧 3.08a **Listen and match.**

2 **Follow and match. Then say.**

Let's build!

Think of something you can do. Draw and share with a friend.

Lesson 5 → Communication

1 What can't they do? Listen and match.

①

②

 **2** Listen and repeat. Then point and say.

3 What can you do? What can't you do? Tell a friend.

color me

26

1 🎧 3.15a **Listen, point, and say.**

a

b

c

d

Clap your hands!

I can shine!

Think and share

2 ✏️ **Look, think, and draw.**

color me

Play a clapping game with a friend.

Extra time?

27

1   Listen and draw. Then color.

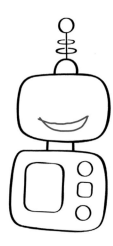

2 Match and say. Then play with a friend.

Look at SB pages 34–35. Who says they can't dance in the story?

Extra time?

3 ✂💬 **Stick and circle. Then tell a friend.**

4 💬 **Think and circle for you. Then tell a friend.**

Make an "I can do it!" poster. Then show and tell your family.

Home-school link

4 Let's eat up

Let's review! SB p32–33 Find and trace. Then say.

h n e

1 Trace and match.

bread

milk

chicken

cheese

olives

tomatoes

bananas

strawberries

Tell me!

Say the words in alphabetical order.

Extra time?

1 Listen and check (✓) or put an ✗.

2 Trace. Then read and draw ☺ or ☹.

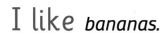 I like *bananas.*

I like *bread.*

I don't like *tomatoes.*

I don't like *chicken.*

I can shine!

3 Color the food you like in Activity 2. Then draw the food you don't like. Tell a friend.

color me

Say your favorite food word.

Extra time?

1 SB p44–45 **Look and find. Then check (✓) the food you see together.**

 +  ☐ **2**  +  ☐

 +  ☐

Let's imagine!

2 **Listen and find. Then color.**
4.07a

I can shine!

3 **Draw. Then say.**

And you? What's your favorite food at school?

color me

Rate the story and tell a friend. ☆☆☆   **Extra time?**

1 ✏️ Trace. Then look and write.

1 [d] I like sandwiches.   2 [ ] I like pizza.

3 [ ] I don't like milkshakes.   4 [ ] I don't like ice cream.

2 💬 Follow and find. Trace and circle for Elena. Then say.

Let's build!

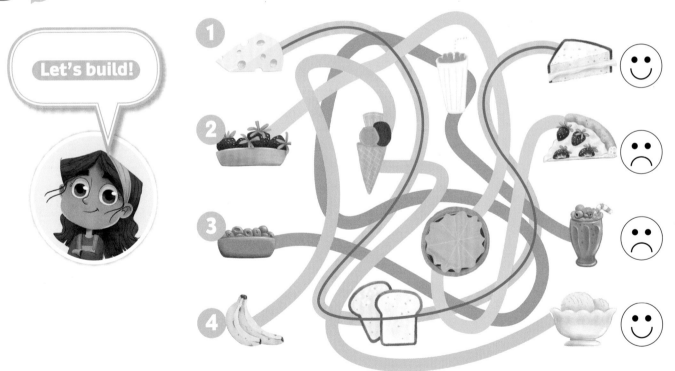

1 **Do you like cheese sandwiches?**
Yes, I do. / No, I don't.

2 **Do you like strawberry pizza?**
Yes, I do. / No, I don't.

3 **Do you like olive milkshakes?**
Yes, I do. / No, I don't.

4 **Do you like banana ice cream?**
Yes, I do. / No, I don't.

Think of your favorite sandwich. Draw and share with a friend.

Extra time?

1 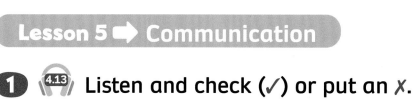 Listen and check (✓) or put an ✗.

My sounds

2 🎧 4.14 ✏️ Listen and repeat. Then color "ch" words blue and "h" words red.

I can shine!

3 ✏️ 💬 Draw the food you like. Ask and answer. Then draw for a friend.

Do you like bread?

Yes, I do.

color me

1 **Circle four differences. Then say.**

1

2

> *Picture 1.*
> *Pasta.*

I can shine!

Think and share

2 4.17a **Listen and circle. Then role-play.**

> *Can I have some... , please?*

color me

Guess your friend's favorite food.

Extra time?

1 🎧 4.17b ✏️ Listen and draw.

2 💬 Trace and match to make your own food.
Then ask and answer.

1 cheese   ice cream

2 olives   milkshakes

3 bananas   sandwiches

4 strawberries   pizza

Do you like... ?

*Yes, I do./
No, I don't.*

Which food is very cold?   **Extra time?**

3 Stick, draw, and color.
Then play the game.

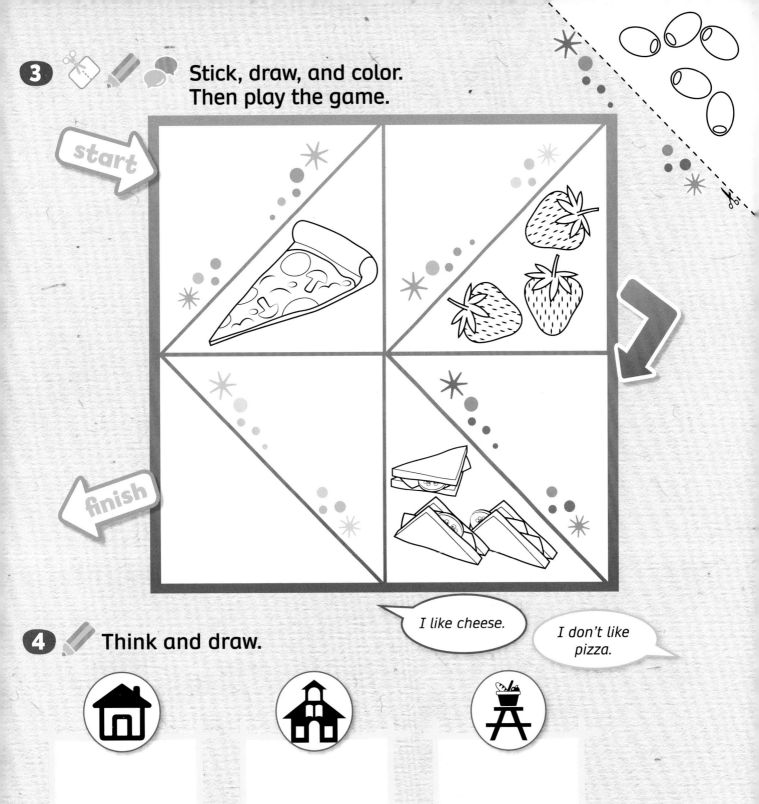

start

finish

I like cheese.

I don't like pizza.

4 Think and draw.

Make a picnic basket. Then show and tell your family.

Review 2 All about me

1 🎧 4.19 **Listen and follow. Then check (✓).**

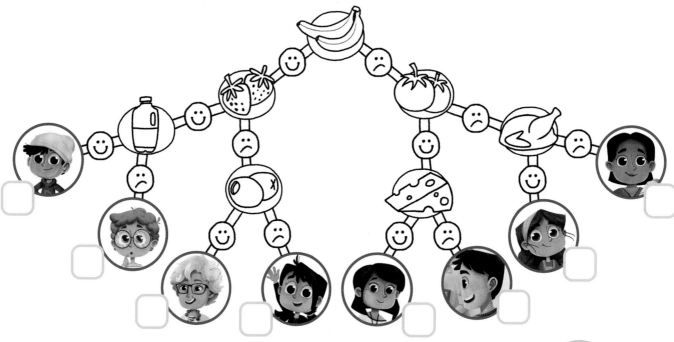

2 **Trace. Then look at Activity 1 and match.**

1 *I like* bananas. *I like* strawberries. *I don't like* milk.

2 *I don't like* bananas. *I don't like* tomatoes. *I like* chicken.

3 💬 **Ask and answer.**

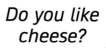
Do you like cheese?

Do you like olives?

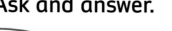
Yes, I do.

No, I don't.

4 Look and check (✓) for you. Then role-play.

Can I have some pizza, please?

Mini-project

6 Think of a pet for you. What can your pet do? Draw and say.

5 Trace. Then look and match.

1 FACT SHEET

I have 4 legs *and 2 big ears. I can* run.

2 FACT SHEET

I have small eyes. *I can* hop.

Time to shine!

7 Look, think, and color.

1  ✓ ? ✗

2 ✓ ? ✗

3 ✓ ? ✗

5 Nature around us

Lesson 1 ➡ Vocabulary

Let's review! SB p42-43 ➡ Find and trace. Then say.

 b 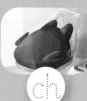 ch  t

1 Look, trace, and match.

owl

frog

rabbit

lizard

duck

turtle

fox

mouse

Tell me!

40

Say the words in alphabetical order.

Extra time?

1 🎧 5.06 Listen and check (✓) or put an ✗.

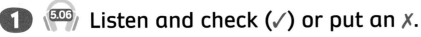

1 ✓   2 ☐   3 ☐   4 ☐

2 🎧 5.06a Count and match. Then listen and check.

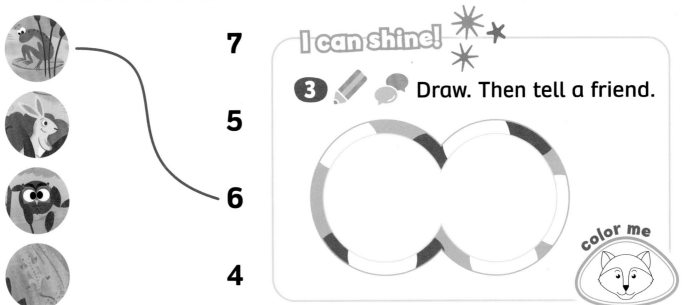

7

5

6

4

I can shine!

3 ✏️ 💬 Draw. Then tell a friend.

color me

Say your favorite animal word.

Extra time?

1 SB p 56-57 ➡ **Circle the one that doesn't belong.**

1  **2**  **3**  **4**

2 ✏ **Connect the dots. Then color.**

Let's imagine!
I can see
a butterfly.

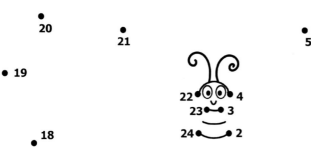
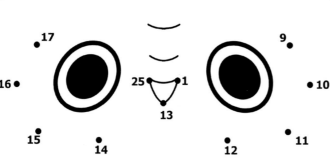

20
21
5
6

19
22 4
23 3
7

18
24 2
8

17
9

16
25 1
10

13

15
14
12
11

I can shine!

3 ✏ **Draw. Then say.**

And you? Can you
see a big animal?

color me

Rate the story and tell a friend. ☆☆☆

Extra time?

1   **Listen and trace. Then ask and answer.**

1 Is it a ladybug? Yes, it is./No, it isn't.
2 Is it a bee? Yes, it is./No, it isn't.

2 **Follow and find. Then say.**

Let's build!

Which animals are at the park?

3 **Trace. Then look and match.**

ladybug
ant
butterfly
bee

Think of your favorite small animal. Draw and share with a friend.

Extra time?

43

1 🎧 **5.13** Listen and trace.

My sounds

2 🎧 **5.14** Listen and repeat. Trace. Then check (✓) the one that doesn't belong.

I can shine!

3 💬✏️ Ask and answer with a friend. Then draw.

Is it a/an... ?

Yes, it is.

color me

1 Trace. Is it their home?
Check (✓) or put an ✗.

Look at
the frog.

1 pond ✓

2 flowers

3 tree

4 grass

I can shine!

Think and share
Think about a park close
to you. Can you find a
pond with ducks or frogs?

2 🖍 💬 Look at Activity 1. Choose and draw
an animal in its home. Tell a friend.

Look at
the animal!

color me

What can you see in your classroom? Tell a friend.

Extra
time?

1 Trace. Then look, count, and match.

frog   **1**

lizard   **2**

mouse   **3**

turtle   **4**

fox   **5**

owl   **6**

rabbit   **7**

duck   **8**

2 Ask and answer. Then connect the dots and say.

Is it a bee?

No, it isn't.

What can you see?

Extra time?

3 ✂️ ✏️ 💬 **Stick and color. Then tell a friend.**

I can see one fox.

It's a butterfly.

4 ✏️ 💬 **Think and draw. Then tell a friend.**

Make an origami owl. Then show and tell your family.

Home-school link

6 Let's dress up

Let's review! SB p54–55 ➡ **Find and write. Then say.**

d

1 **Look and write.**

| shirt | pants | sweater | shoes | dress | shorts | T-shirt | ~~pajamas~~ |

pajamas

Tell me!

Look at my new words. Match and color.

a Clothes

b Nature

Say the words in alphabetical order.

Extra time?

1 🎧 ✏️ **Listen and color.**

2 ✏️ **Look at Activity 1. Then read and write.**

shoes ~~shorts~~ pants shirt

1 I'm wearing purple __shorts__.

2 I'm wearing black _____.

3 I'm wearing pink _____.

4 I'm wearing a blue _____.

I can shine!

3 💬 **Check (✓) and say. Then tell a friend.**

I'm wearing... .

pajamas ☐
a T-shirt ☐
a dress ☐
pants ☐
shoes ☐
a sweater ☐

color me

Write your favorite clothes word. _____

1 SB p66–67 **Who is happy? Look and circle.**

2 **Find and color.
Then say.**

Let's imagine!

I'm wearing a purple sweater/ T-shirt, black shoes, and blue pants/shorts.

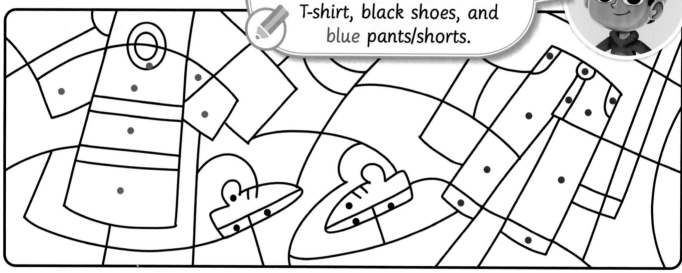

 I can shine!

3 **Draw and color.
Write for you.
Then say.**

I'm wearing
_____.

color me

Rate the story and tell a friend. ☆☆☆

Extra time?

1 **Trace. Then read and number.**

1  I'm hot.

2 I'm happy.

3 I'm sad.

4 I'm cold.

Let's build!

What are you wearing?

2 **Read and write.**

~~cold~~ hot sad happy

1 I'm wearing pajamas. I'm _____cold_____.

2 I'm wearing my favorite dress. I'm _____.

3 I'm wearing two sweaters. I'm _____.

4 I'm wearing a yellow T-shirt. I don't like yellow. I'm

_____. But I have a red jumper. I like red!

Think of your favorite clothes. Draw and share with a friend.

Extra time?

1 🎧 6.13 Listen and check (✓).

My sounds

2 🎧 6.14 ✏️ Listen and repeat. Trace.
Then color "j" words blue
and "sh" words green.

I can shine!

3 ✏️ & 💬 Color clothes for a cold day. Write.
Then tell a friend.

I'm wearing
_____
and _____.

color me

1 Look and write. Then say.

boots   skirt   sun hat   ~~jeans~~

1    **2**    **3**    **4**

jeans   _____   _____   _____

I'm wearing jeans.

Think and share

Think about a festival. Do you dress up with your friends?

I can shine!

2 Draw special clothes for your friend. Write. Then role-play.

Wear _____ and _____!

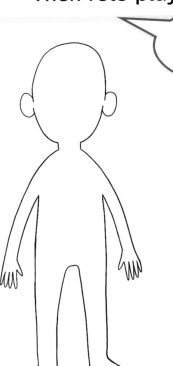

color me

What are your favorite special clothes? Tell a friend.

Extra time?

1 ✏️ **Trace and write.**

> pants   shorts   a shirt   ~~a T-shirt~~
> shoes   pajamas   a dress   a sweater

I'm wearing
__a T-shirt__ ,
_____ ,
and
_____ .

I'm wearing
_____ ,
_____ ,
and
_____ .

2 **Trace and match. Then role-play.**

I'm sad.   I'm hot.

 ①

 ②

③

④

I'm cold.   I'm happy.

What's this? It's a ___ ___ ___ .

Extra time?

3 Stick, draw, and color.
Then play the game.

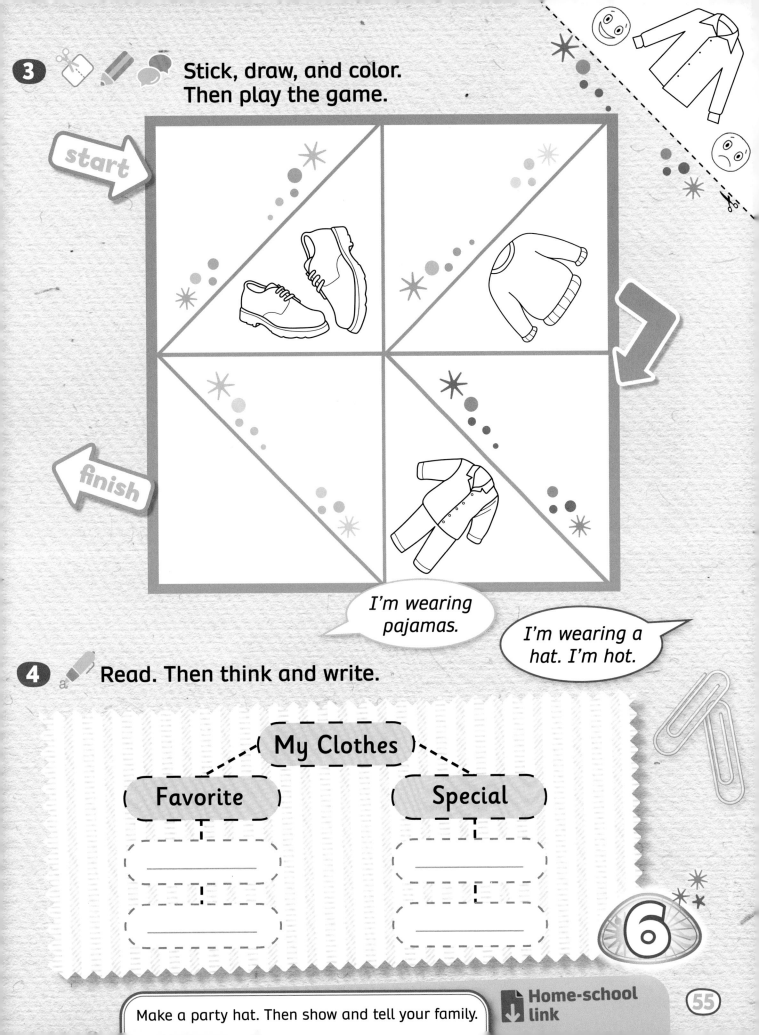

start

finish

I'm wearing pajamas.

I'm wearing a hat. I'm hot.

4 Read. Then think and write.

My Clothes

Favorite

Special

Make a party hat. Then show and tell your family.

Review 3 Around me

1 Find and circle five differences.

2 6.19 Listen and check (✓).

3 Look at Activity 1. Trace. Then read and number.

I'm wearing shorts.
I can see a mouse.

I'm wearing a dress.
I can see a lizard.

4 Play *Which picture?* with a friend.

I'm wearing jeans.
I can see a frog.

Is it Picture 2?

Yes, it is.

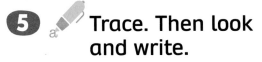

5 Trace. Then look and write.

| sad   hot   happy |

1

I'm wearing
pajamas.
I'm _____ .

2

I'm wearing pants
and a sweater.
I'm _____ .

3

I'm wearing
a shirt.
I'm _____ .

Mini-project

6  Draw clothes for your friend's costume party. Then write and say.

Time to shine!

7 Read and color.

1 I can write animal words.

2 I can write clothes words.

3 I can talk about what's around me.

4 I completed Review 3!

Goodbye from Rise and Shine Towers

1   Trace. Then write and say.

I can see a... .

 book

 pencil

 flower

 door

 tree

 bird

 bag

 ball

School ____ book ____ **Park**

____ ____ ____

____ ____ ____

2   Listen and number.

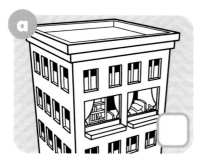

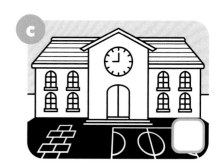

3 Trace. Then circle.

It's a school.
I can see books / flowers.

It's a park.
I can see desks / trees.

4 **Look and write. Then point, ask, and answer.**

Is it a/an... ?

Yes, it is./ No, it isn't.

1

2

3

music-box
strawberries
elephant
bird party
rabbit

<u>music box</u>

_____

_____

4

5

6

_____

_____

_____

   5 `7.06` **Trace. Then sing.**

Goodbye!
Have a great
vacation!

It's fall!

1 🎧 8.04 ✏️ Trace and match. Then listen and color.

tree leaf apple chestnut pumpkin fire

Winter vacation

2 🎧 8.08 Trace and match. Then listen and number.

hat gloves scarf boots snow lights

Spring is here!

3 🎧 8.12 Trace. Then listen and number.

(egg) (blossom) (chick) (lamb) (flower) (rabbit)

Sunny summer days

4 🎧 8.16 Trace. Then listen and circle.

I'm wearing my
(sun hat) / swimsuit.
I'm wearing a sun hat / sunglasses, too.
All ready to play,
On a sunny / picnic, summer day.

I'm wearing my
swimsuit / sunglasses.
We have a beach / picnic lunch.
Let's have an ice cream each,
And go to the picnic / beach!

Picture Dictionary

Welcome

Vocabulary

 bag
 book
 chair
 desk
 door
 pencil

Unit 1

Vocabulary 1

 ball
 car
 doll
 elephant

 robot
 tablet
 teddy bear
 train

Vocabulary 2

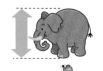 big
 new

 old
 small

Unit 2

Vocabulary 1

aunt
brother
dad
grandpa

grandma
mom
sister
uncle

Vocabulary 2

bird
cat

hamster
fish

Unit 3

Vocabulary 1

 arms

 ears

 eyes

 feet

 hands

 legs

 mouth

 nose

Vocabulary 2

 dance

 hop

 jump

 run

Unit 4

Vocabulary 1

 bananas

 bread

 cheese

 chicken

 milk

 olives

 strawberries

 tomatoes

Vocabulary 2

 ice cream

 milkshake

 pizza

 sandwiches

Unit 5

Vocabulary 1

 duck

 fox

 frog

 lizard

 mouse

 owl

 rabbit

 turtle

Vocabulary 2

 ant

 bee

 butterfly

 ladybug

Vocabulary 1

 dress

 sweater

 pajamas

 shirt

 shoes

 shorts

 pants

T-shirt

Vocabulary 2

 cold

 happy

 hot

 sad

Fall

Vocabulary

 apple

 chestnut

 fire

 leaf

 pumpkin

 tree

Winter

Vocabulary

 boots

 gloves

 hat

 lights

 scarf

 snow

Spring

Vocabulary

 blossom

 chick

 egg

 flower

 lamb

 rabbit

Summer

Vocabulary

 beach

 picnic

 sunglasses

 sun hat

 sunny

 swimsuit